W H A L E

W H A L E

Giant of the Ocean

Eric S. Grace

LP LONGMEADOW PRESS

First published in Canada by Key Porter Books Limited, 1996.

PAGE 1: AFTER 12 MONTHS OF GESTATION, A HUMPBACK WHALE PRODUCES A 15-FOOT (4.5-M)-LONG CALF WEIGHING ABOUT 1½ TONS (1.5 T). SHE MAY MATE AGAIN SOON AFTER GIVING BIRTH.

PAGES 2-3: THE SIGHT OF DOLPHINS LEAPING AHEAD OF THE WAVES BRINGS MUCH PLEASURE TO SIGHTSEERS TRAVELING AT SEA. THE BEST VIEW OF THESE SMALLER CETACEANS IS OFTEN HAD WHEN THEY COME TO RIDE THE SURGE OF WATER AT THE BOW OF A SHIP.

PAGE 4: DIVER MEETS HUMPBACKS. IN SPITE OF ALL OUR TECHNOLOGY, HUMANS CAN ONLY BE TEMPORARY VISITORS IN THE WHALES' UNDERWATER WORLD.

PAGE 5: A HUMPBACK FLIPS ITS TAIL INTO THE AIR AS IT ROLLS INTO A DEEP DIVE. THESE WHALES MAY STAY UNDERWATER BETWEEN BREATHS FOR UP TO HALF AN HOUR.

Cover and interior design: Annabelle Stanley
ISBN: 0-681-21499-6
Printed and bound in Hong Kong
First Longmeadow Press Edition, 1996
0 9 8 7 6 5 4 3 2 1

To Kristjan

WHALE

CONTENTS

Beneath the Waves

13

Hunters and Gatherers

33

In the Body of a Whale

57

Family Life

85

Saving the Whales

105

Families of Whales

123

Conservation Groups

124

Selected Bibliography

125

Photography Credits

126

Index

127

BENEATH THE WAVES

"**T**HAR SHE BLOWS!" A CENTURY AND MORE ago, this cry signaled to whalers that heavy work was ahead. Now, a similar call is sending a thrill of anticipation through seafarers of a different generation – those of us who go searching for whales … well … simply for the experience. To feel firsthand what it's like to be in the presence of the largest animals ever to have lived on this planet.

A telltale blowspout hangs briefly over the water, pinpointing the place where one of these elusive giants has broken the seamless surface of waves. The blowspout, a plume of exhaled breath and droplets of sea water, reminds me that the animals we're looking for out here in the ocean near Hawaii are warm-blooded, air-breathing creatures like ourselves. Perhaps some sense of kinship draws us, leaning eagerly across the ship's railing, watching for another glimpse.

Our tiny ship skips nonchalantly across a world that we know less about than the moon. The deep, dark waters covering two-thirds of the earth are unwelcoming

LEFT: A BLOWSPOUT IS OFTEN THE FIRST INDICATION OF A WHALE IN THE DISTANCE. IN THIS CASE, THE PLUME OF WATER VAPOR PINPOINTS AN ORCA TAKING A BREATH OFF VANCOUVER ISLAND.

13

to beings like us, adapted to land underfoot and wind on our skin. We can enter this alien and dangerous realm for only brief moments at a time, fishing out fragments of information about the animals that live there. What do they do down there, those whales, when they're out of our sight? What can we learn from them, whose ancestors, too, once walked on land?

The journey of mammals back to the sea began about 100 million years ago, among a group of animals whose modern descendants also include hoofed mammals, such as deer, horses, pigs, and elephants. By 50 million years ago, adaptations to life in water were well established. Fossils dating back to that period tell us of 6-foot (1.8-m)-long, fish-eating animals that lived by the sea's edge but still spent at least some time on land.

Generation by generation, whales were shaped into creatures totally at home among the rolling, blue-green waves. They lost their ancestors' fur and limbs, not needed in their new way of life. The opening connecting their lungs to the outside air moved to a more efficient position on top of their heads. (An embryo whale starts out with two nostrils at the tip of its snout, like other animals, but its air passage shifts as it develops in the womb.) Their bodies grew larger to conserve heat, and they developed larger jaws to help them capture more food.

Links in the whales' intriguing evolutionary history are still being discovered by scientists every year, in recently uncovered fossil bones and in DNA from modern whales and related species. The evidence shows that most of the different types of whales living today had already appeared by about 20 million years ago.

There's another spout! It hovers in the still air, a bit closer now, off to the starboard side. You can see part of a long, curved back as well, a hint of the massive bulk below. If you could look inside that submerged body, you'd see clues to those long-ago ancestors. Small, bony remains where the hind legs used to be. Muscles that moved ears that no longer exist on the whale's smooth head.

We know quite a lot about whale anatomy, because for years our main interest in whales was carving up their bodies into meat, blubber, and bones. But it's astonishing how little else we know about them. They're difficult to study in the wild, for obvious reasons. The sight of a blowspout, the glimpse of a back or a fin, a few seconds of watching as a tail flips up, then slaps the waves – these are tantalizing rewards for hours of gazing at miles of open water. We know so little about their world that a living species of whale unknown to scientists was discovered as recently as 1992. The fifth new species found since 1937, the 12-foot (3.8-m)- long beaked whale was identified from a few specimens recovered from nets or washed ashore along the coast of Peru.

There are more than 70 species of whales living today, in oceans around the world. They are classified in an order of mammals named Cetàcea, which scientists divide into about 10 different families. Some whales are large, slow-moving, and gentle, like the gray whale. Others are smaller, swift, and agile, like beaked whales, pilot whales, dolphins, and porpoises. Some spend their lives in one small area of ocean, and some migrate during the year over thousands of miles. A few – all dolphins – live in large rivers. Different species of whale eat different foods, from fish, squid, or seals to tiny floating crustaceans.

The animal ahead of our boat off the coast of Maui is a humpback whale. Humpbacks range throughout oceans from the poles to the equator, and some Pacific populations gather here between December and April to breed. You can tell it's a humpback from the appearance of its spout, which is broad and roughly pear shaped. A blue whale's spout is cone shaped and rises straight up about 30 feet (9 m). A sperm whale's spout slants forward and to the left. Right whales have V-shaped spouts. Humpbacks are also distinguished by their enormously long flippers, which are about a third of their total body length of 60 feet (18 m).

Not all whales are this big. Nearly half of all species – most of them dolphins and porpoises – are less than 10 feet (3 m) long when fully grown. But there's no doubt the word *whale* conjures up the truly gigantic. The largest whales are so much bigger than any other animals that it's difficult to relate to them. For example, a blue whale, the biggest of them all, can grow to be 100 feet (30 m) long and weigh as much as a whole herd of elephants (150 tons/136 t). By comparison, estimated weights of the biggest known dinosaurs are no more than a half to a third of this. The blue whale's tongue alone is the weight of an adult elephant. Its heart is the size of a compact automobile, and its arteries are as big around as stovepipes.

Why so big? Living in water has much to do with it. The dense medium supports the whale's body, making it almost weightless. An animal this big on land would collapse under the pull of gravity. The whale's large size also helps it conserve heat in the chilly ocean. A large, warm body loses heat much more slowly than a small, equally warm body, because it has less surface area relative to its mass.

Look there! Quickly! This is the sight we've been hoping for, an unforgettable spectacle dreamed of since long before we left shore. The magnificent animal is breaching – leaping clear out of the water, twisting in the air, and crashing back into the sea with a resounding and astonishing splash. It's a show well worth

16

waiting for. Just imagine the power it takes to propel that 40-ton (36-t) bulk like a rocket into the air. To do that, it must work up a speed of about 25 miles (40 km) per hour, all with a few thrusts of its muscular tail. Is the whale leaping for fun? Is it setting off sound waves to tell other whales "I'm here"? Maybe it's simply relieving an itchy skin or trying to dislodge clinging pests.

It's rather a cliché to have a big, brawny guy be a gentle and peace-loving softy, yet there's truth in this paradox. Whales, for all their size and strength, are remarkably inoffensive to humans who invade their world. The mighty tail we just saw slipping beneath the waves could easily flip over a small boat without even trying, but whales are rarely aggressive toward people, even those who persecute them. They sometimes seem interested in us, and there are many stories of whales helping swimmers in distress and saving their lives.

Here's one account of close encounters with gray whales: "A big female, three times as long as our dinghy, swam under us and lifted the dinghy on her head. She took us for a short ride before letting us down. Another time, one of them blew bubbles under the boat – it felt as if someone were hitting the bottom of the boat with rocks. One whale swam up beside us and, while still a few inches under water, blasted air out of its blowhole, giving us a cold shower. I think it liked to hear us scream."

Some whales, especially young ones, seem to enjoy playing with people, sometimes for hours at a time. Unlike other wild animals, they freely approach people without being bribed with food. Why they should do this nobody knows, but evidence suggests that whales have a curiosity and intelligence that rival our own.

Both whales and people have long lifespans; live in cooperative social groupings;

use sophisticated vocal communication; have large, complex brains; and are able to learn new skills very quickly. But whales differ from us in two profoundly important ways: they live in the oceans, and they do not have hands to build and make things. Our hands, as much as our brains, have allowed us to manipulate and dominate much of the world around us. What might whales do with such a gift if they had it?

Meeting the alien wisdom of whales on their own ground helps bring some humility to human ambition. For all our technology we can only ever be temporary visitors in the ocean, in many ways a far harder region to explore than outer space. Yet whales – relatives of ours if you go back far enough – are as blithely ascendant out here as we are on land. They are fascinating, beautiful, awesome, and elusive creatures, deserving every bit of our respect and care. It's the least we can do for an animal that's able to thrill us simply by breathing out.

RIGHT: A YOUNG GRAY WHALE APPEARS TO ENJOY BEING PATTED AND STROKED. THESE GENTLE GIANTS MAY PLAY WITH WHALE WATCHERS FOR AN HOUR OR MORE AT A TIME.

A SIGHT ALL WHALE WATCHERS HOPE TO SEE, A HUMPBACK WHALE BEGINS TO BREACH,

RISING OUT OF THE WATER IN A HIGH LEAP...

...THEN ARCHING INTO A BACKWARD FLIP BEFORE CRASHING BACK INTO THE WATER.

OPPOSITE: HUMPBACK WHALES SOMETIMES LIE MOTIONLESS ON THE SURFACE,

WITH ONE LONG FLIPPER HOISTED LIKE A SAIL. ON OCCASION, THEY SLAP THE

WATER HARD WITH THEIR FLIPPERS, MAKING A NOISE LIKE A RIFLE SHOT.

ABOVE: A BELUGA LEAPS ABOVE A CALM STRETCH OF WATER AMONG THE ICE

FLOES. LIVING YEAR-ROUND IN THE ARCTIC, THESE SMALL, PLUMP WHALES ARE

EASILY IDENTIFIED BY THEIR WHITE COLOR AND LACK OF DORSAL FIN.

OPPOSITE: WHALE WATCHERS LEAN EAGERLY OVER THE SIDE OF THEIR DINGHY TO SEE A GRAY WHALE SWIMMING CALMLY BESIDE THEM. THOUSANDS OF THESE WHALES MIGRATE EACH YEAR ALONG THE SHALLOW COASTAL WATERS BETWEEN ALASKA AND BAJA CALIFORNIA.

᷈᭰

ABOVE: TWO PHOTOGRAPHERS ARE DWARFED BY THE MASSIVE HEAD OF A GRAY WHALE BLOWING BUBBLES NEAR THE SURFACE, ALMOST UNDER THEIR DINGHY.

SEA LIONS, SEALS, AND WALRUS, LIKE WHALES,
EVOLVED FROM ANCESTORS LIVING ON LAND. THEY
FEED AND TRAVEL IN THE OCEANS BUT RETURN TO
LAND TO BREED AND SUCKLE THEIR YOUNG.

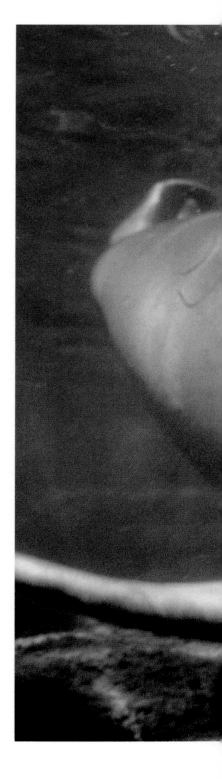

PILOT WHALES ARE SLENDER MEMBERS OF THE DOLPHIN FAMILY. FOUND IN WARMER

OCEANS, THEY TRAVEL IN LARGE GROUPS, SOMETIMES IN THE COMPANY OF

OTHER DOLPHIN SPECIES.

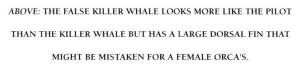

ABOVE: THE FALSE KILLER WHALE LOOKS MORE LIKE THE PILOT
THAN THE KILLER WHALE BUT HAS A LARGE DORSAL FIN THAT
MIGHT BE MISTAKEN FOR A FEMALE ORCA'S.

LEFT: THE MELONHEAD IS A SMALL WHALE, UNDER 10 FEET (3 M)
LONG. IT RESEMBLES THE PILOT WHALE AND PYGMY KILLER
WHALE, BUT LITTLE IS KNOWN ABOUT IT, AND SCIENTISTS ARE
UNCERTAIN HOW TO CLASSIFY IT.

HUNTERS AND GATHERERS

Jack Spratt could eat no fat;
His wife could eat no lean.
And so, between the two of them,
They licked the platter clean.

LIKE THE COUPLE IN THE NURSERY RHYME, whales are separated into two distinct groups that seem to have divided the sea's banquet between them. One group of whales feeds mainly on tiny, floating organisms suspended in the surface waters, and the other group dines only on larger prey, mostly fish and squid.

Odd as it may seem, the biggest whales thrive on the smallest food – the drifting fish eggs, larvae, small jellyfish, and shrimp that make up part of the plankton. To take advantage of this abundant food supply, their mouths have been modified into massive sieves. Instead of teeth, which they don't need, they have vertical rows of comblike structures growing from the roofs of their mouths. These struc-

LEFT: AN ORCA LAUNCHES ITSELF ONTO THE BEACH IN PATAGONIA TO SNATCH A SEA LION, WHICH IT TOSSES

IN THE AIR. ALMOST ANYTHING IN THE SEA IS AT RISK FROM THESE STEALTHY AND INTELLIGENT PREDATORS.

tures are filtering plates, made from a flexible, horny material called baleen, or whalebone. Each has fine bristles along one edge, making overlapping fringes that trap food from the water.

There are 10 species of plankton-feeders or baleen whales, a group that scientists name Mysticetes (meaning whales with mustaches). Their baleen plates vary in size and appearance, ranging from 1 foot (0.3 m) to 15 feet (4.5 m) in length, and from 150 to 700 in number.

Different baleen whales use different techniques to gather their food from the ocean. Some of them, such as right whales and bowhead whales, are skimmers. They swim slowly near the surface with their cavelike mouths open, sifting out plankton as it flows through their jaws. They have long baleen plates and enormous heads. The head of a bowhead whale, for example, is more than a third of its body length and as tall as a two-story building, with a highly arched palate and scooplike lower jaws.

Other baleen whales are gulpers. Their heads are smaller, but their throats are pleated so they can expand, like a pelican's pouch. They have shorter, wider baleen plates with long fringes that can capture slightly larger prey. They feed by lunging into thick gatherings of plankton and small fish with their mouths open, gulping in as much as 4 tons (3.6 t) of this sea soup in one go. With their mouths full and jaws closed, they force water out through the baleen by contracting their throats and pushing up their tongues. Food left behind on the frilled edges of the baleen is then swallowed. These whales are also known as rorquals, from a Norwegian term meaning "tubed whale." They are graceful, streamlined, powerful swimmers and include blue whales, fin whales, sei whales, and humpbacks.

Humpbacks sometimes use a clever tactic to corral small fish or shrimp into a tighter group before gulping them down. They do this by circling underneath their prey while blowing out a steady stream of air bubbles. Confused and frightened, the little animals move toward the center of this bubble net, which the whale gradually draws tighter before swimming up and taking its reward.

Gray whales, another baleen species, have a third feeding technique. They forage on the ocean floor in shallow coastal waters, digging grooves in the sediment with their narrow jaws, then sucking in the stirred-up mixture of mud and bottom-dwelling organisms. They have a short baleen with coarse bristles, which lets the fine sediment out but keeps crustaceans, molluscs, and tube-worms in. You can tell where a group of gray whales has recently been feeding because the sea water in their wake appears murky, like a river estuary after a flood.

The majority of whale species – more than 85 percent – are not plankton-feeders but hunters. They are named Odontocetes (meaning whales with teeth). Most are smaller than baleen whales and are speedier swimmers, designed to pursue fast-moving prey. About half are species of dolphins or porpoises. The largest toothed whales are sperm whales, which may be more than 60 feet (18 m) in length, followed by killer whales, with a maximum length of about 30 feet (9 m).

Like the Mysticetes, the Odontocetes vary in their feeding habits. Most eat fish, but some specialize in catching squid, and one species (killer whales) feeds on sea mammals. For the most part, their teeth are all cone shaped, used to grab and hold their slippery prey before swallowing it whole or tearing off chunks. They do not chew their food.

Whales grow only one set of teeth, the size and number depending on the

the sperm whale tearing at the soft, heavy body of the squid with its powerful teeth, while the victim clamps on to its attacker, ripping the whale's flesh with its beak and probing for eyes and blowhole with its tentacles. Many sperm whales bear round scars on their skin, left by suckers an inch (2.5 cm) or more across.

To pursue their prey, great sperm whales have become champion divers. They regularly descend more than 3,000 feet (900 m) to hunt, and have even been recorded below 7,000 feet (2130 m). More amazing still, they can descend at a speed of about 4 knots (4 nautical miles or 7 km per hour) and surface twice as fast. A round trip to 3,300 feet (1000 m) at this rate would take a sperm whale no more than 15 minutes. They usually return to the surface close to the spot where they went down, suggesting that their underwater journeys are largely vertical.

Sperm whales can not only dive deep and fast, but also they often remain submerged for long periods at a time – 45 minutes or so. Given that they can get to and from their hunting depths much more quickly than this, and that they don't swim far from their diving point, it seems that their strategy is to descend to the target depth, then wait motionless in ambush for a passing squid.

Anatomical evidence supports this exciting image. A sperm whale has huge nasal passages (up to 15 feet/4.5 m long and 3 feet/0.9 m across), which run from its blowhole through a reservoir of spermaceti wax in the whale's head.

Specializing in deep-sea squid, sperm whales share this abundant but difficult-to-get supply of food with beaked whales. As with all animals, their dependence on what they eat affects other areas of their lives. Only full-grown bulls can capture the largest squid, consuming up to a ton of squid per adult whale per day.

Cows and calves, on the other hand, eat smaller squid and fish at shallower depths. Because of this difference in feeding habits, the two sexes lead different lives. Females and young whales remain in temperate waters all year round, but adult males travel long distances throughout the year, moving from tropical waters to subpolar regions each summer and returning each winter. One explanation for these movements is that the bulls are following the breeding migration of the giant squid. Unable, perhaps, to survive for long on smaller fare, they must go where their food goes.

Giant baleen whales, too, are slaves to their tiny prey. They depend for their survival on areas of ocean where plankton thrive in large enough quantities to fuel their massive needs. The only waters of the world where this occurs are near the poles – and there only in the summer when waters are temperate.

Biological productivity in the oceans, unlike on land, is greater in polar regions than in the tropics. There are several reasons for this. First, cold water holds more dissolved gases than warm water. This means there's plenty of oxygen for respiration, and carbon dioxide for photosynthesis. Second, polar oceans receive extra rations of sunshine during their summer months. The earth's angle of tilt points each pole in turn toward the sun for half a year at a time, giving first one pole then the other a season of continuous daylight. Third, the Arctic and Antarctic regions benefit from a mixing of cold and warm waters. Ocean water cooled by ice sinks and moves outward from the poles along the sea floor, while warmer waters from the tropics flow in the opposite direction. Where they meet, the warm currents well up over the cold like plumes of smoke, carrying with them nutrients from decomposing organisms that would otherwise sink and remain on

RIGHT: A KILLER WHALE, OR ORCA, HAS A MOUTHFUL OF LARGE CONE-SHAPED TEETH.

IT CANNOT CHEW PREY BUT SWALLOWS IT WHOLE OR RIPS OFF LARGE CHUNKS.

🐋

BELOW: PARALLEL SCARS ON THE SKIN OF A GRAY WHALE ARE SOUVENIRS OF A

PAST ESCAPE FROM THE TEETH OF AN ORCA. GROUPS OF ORCAS SOMETIMES ATTACK

LARGER WHALES, BUT DO NOT USUALLY KILL FULL-GROWN ONES.

A GRAY WHALE WASHED UP ON A BEACH NEAR VANCOUVER SHOWS THE ROWS OF COMBLIKE

BALEEN PLATES LINING ITS HUGE MOUTH. CLUSTERS OF BARNACLES FORM WHITE PATCHES

OVER ITS HEAD. THESE SMALL RIDERS ATTACH THEMSELVES TO LARGE, SLOW WHALES, AS THEY

DO TO THE HULLS OF SHIPS, BUT DO NOT SEEM TO HARM THE WHALES.

BLUE WHALES AND OTHER BALEEN WHALES ARE SOMETIMES CALLED RORQUALS, FROM A

NORWEGIAN WORD DESCRIBING THE RIBBED APPEARANCE OF THEIR THROATS. AFTER FILLING

THEIR THROAT POUCHES WITH "SEA SOUP," THEY FORCE OUT THE WATER, TRAPPING SHRIMP,

FISH, AND OTHER ANIMALS ON THE BALEEN PLATES IN THEIR MOUTHS.

ABOVE: HUMPBACKS FEED BY LUNGING FORWARD AT THE SURFACE WITH THEIR MOUTHS OPEN, SCOOPING UP WATER WITH SMALL

FISH OR CRUSTACEANS. THE DISTINCTIVE GROOVES ALONG THE THROAT ARE PLEATS THAT ALLOW THE THROAT CAVITY TO EXPAND.

❧

OPPOSITE: KRILL, MEASURING ONLY 1 OR 2 INCHES (2.5 TO 5 CM) IN LENGTH, ARE THE MAIN FOOD OF BALEEN WHALES. THEY BLOOM

EACH SUMMER IN THE ANTARCTIC OCEAN, FORMING THICK RAFTS SEVERAL ACRES IN AREA.

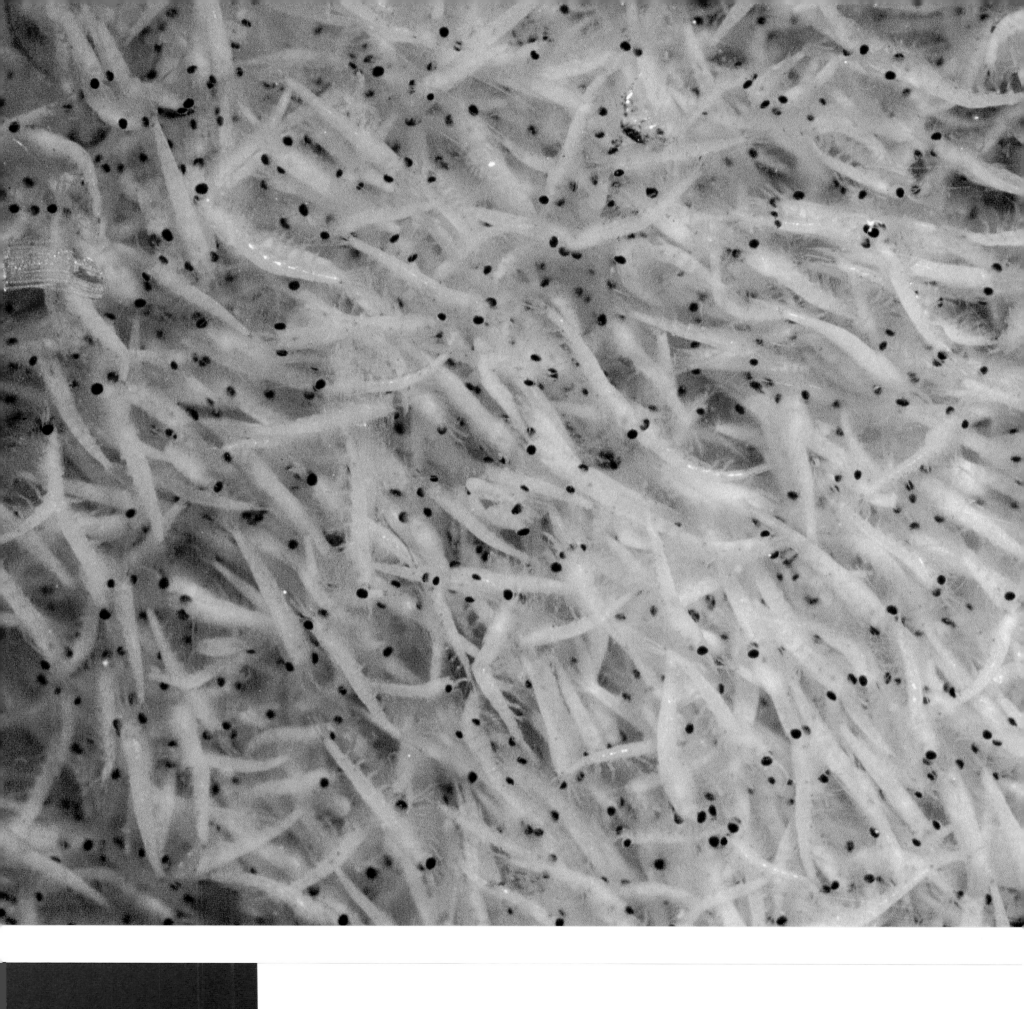

ABOVE: THE MINKE IS THE SMALLEST OF THE RORQUAL WHALES, MEASURING ABOUT

30 FEET (9 M) LONG WHEN FULLY GROWN. ITS SMALL, POINTED DORSAL FIN IS IN THE

LAST THIRD OF THE BACK. ALTHOUGH IT IS A BALEEN WHALE, THE MINKE EATS MORE FISH

THAN THE OTHER FILTER-FEEDING WHALES.

ABOVE: PYGMY KILLER WHALES FEED ON SMALL FISH MOSTLY AT NIGHT AND SPEND SUNNY DAYS LOAFING AT THE SURFACE.

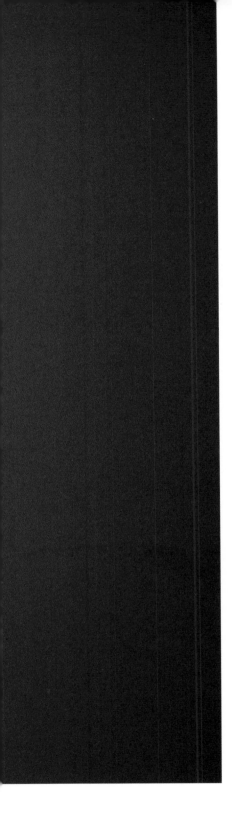

BELOW: A 100 (101-T)-TON BLUE WHALE MAKES

A SIZABLE SPLASH AFTER BREACHING.

OPPOSITE: HUMPBACK WHALES SOMETIMES

USE STREAMS OF BUBBLES TO TRAP THEIR

PREY. THEY CIRCLE BELOW SCHOOLS OF SMALL

FISH OR SHRIMP, PRODUCING A CURTAIN OF

BUBBLES THAT SCARES THE ANIMALS INTO A

TIGHT GROUP FOR THE WHALE TO GULP.

IN THE BODY
OF A WHALE

CHESAPEAKE BAY, SPRING 1942. ENEMY submarines were in the Atlantic, and underwater listening devices, newly developed by the U.S. Navy, had picked up alarming noises. Eerie sounds, like a hundred pneumatic drills smashing through pavement, put the navy on alert and sent warning phone calls speeding to Washington. As it turned out, the navy need not have worried. The noisy invaders were croaker fish, not submarines.

The discovery that oceans are noisy should not really have been so surprising. After all, sound travels through water much more readily than through air. And seafarers in the days of sailing ships knew the songs of whales and told stories of strange, ghostly sounds at sea. Decades of rumbling, powered ships had drowned out generations of memories, however, altering the common perception of oceans so that they became regarded as silent worlds of underwater life. With wartime technology, the voices of the sea were heard again, in new and thrilling detail.

LEFT: BELUGAS, OR WHITE WHALES, SWIM IN A SLOW AND STATELY FASHION NEAR THE SURFACE. EARLY MARINERS CALLED THEM "SEA CANARIES" BECAUSE OF THEIR LOUD WHISTLES AND SQUEALS.

Navy hydrophones opened up a world vibrant with the grunts, squeaks, whistles, groans, and chirps of fish, crustaceans, and whales.

Whales rely on hearing more than any other sense, and for good reason. Eyesight is of limited use in the ocean. It's difficult to see beyond 200 feet (61 m) in even the clearest surface waters, and visibility gets worse as you dive deeper. At 30 feet (9 m) down, about 90 percent of the sunlight hitting the water's surface has been filtered out. Below about 1,500 feet (457 m), it is pitch-black. The sense of sight is even less useful at night, although whales appear to have adaptations for nocturnal vision. Like cats' eyes, whales' eyes shine when struck by light, and they have plenty of light-sensitive rod cells in the retina at the back of each eye.

The sense of smell is likewise limited, having all but disappeared from whales, despite the fact that odors carry far in water and many fish have keen noses. Whales, being mammals and not fish, cannot sniff waterborne smells without getting their lungs full of water. But studies have shown that whales may be able to taste things, despite the fact that they have no olfactory nerves.

Given the murky medium they live in, then, whales have developed a remarkable sensory system based on making and listening to sounds. They make high-pitched sounds (inaudible to our ears) to help them identify relatively close objects, and lower-pitched sounds to communicate over distances of many miles when they are well out of sight of one another. Because understanding the role of sound is important to understanding whales, we'll look at it here in some detail.

The use of sound for "seeing" is best developed in the hunters – the toothed whales. When searching for prey, Odontocetes send out pulses of high-frequency clicks as they swim, then listen to the echoes that come back as the sound waves bounce off objects in their path. It's a very efficient technique. Sound travels almost a mile (1.6 km) a second through water – more than four times faster than in air. With few barriers in the way, sound waves can also travel very far under water. Using its echolocation or sonar system (*sound navigation ranging*), a hunting whale can detect a school of fish a mile (1.6 km) away in two seconds – one second for its click to travel to the fish, one second for the echo to travel back to the whale.

The precise way that whales produce and project their sounds is still a bit of a mystery. They do not have vocal cords but an elaborate system of cavities in their skulls to amplify and focus sound waves created by moving air. With their blowholes shut, they generate sounds in the enclosed air spaces by vibrating their nasal plugs, larynx, or muscles in other parts of the system. The sound waves move forward from the nasal passages, through the head, and out into the surrounding water.

In the front part of their heads, many whales have a lens-shaped structure rich in fat and oil. In Odontocetes this structure, called a melon, is thought to focus sound waves reflected off the curved bone of the skull, producing a concentrated beam of sound. The melon is particularly well developed in sperm whales, which dive deep into the lightless ocean abyss to find their food.

Whales can pick up incoming sound waves through all parts of their bodies. Their ear openings, which in any case are not well positioned to hear sounds coming from in front, are unimportant for hearing under water. They have been reduced to tiny holes, in some cases plugged with wax. The main channel for sound waves reaching the inner ear is along the jawbones in Odontocetes.

Because its bones conduct sound waves, a whale could potentially be confused about the direction of a particular sound source. Vibrations through its skull might blur the information, making it seem as if noise is coming from all around. To overcome this problem, the bones next to a whale's inner ears are isolated from the rest of the skull inside pockets of connective tissue. This allows each ear to function independently of the other, giving the whale a finely tuned stereo sound sense.

Whales produce a wide variety of sounds, from high-frequency clicks at rates of up to 1,000 per second to low-frequency moans lasting up to 30 seconds each. Each sound probably has a different purpose, although we still know very little about their exact function in the whales' lives. In general, the very high-frequency notes, produced only by Odontocetes, are used for food-finding and navigation, while the lower frequencies, produced by all whales, serve for both echolocation in bowheads, and communication.

Here's how it works. The distance a sound travels depends mainly on its wavelength, or frequency. A low-frequency sound (like a deep moan), with a wavelength of, say, 250 feet (76 m), can travel hundreds of miles. These long, sinuous sound waves pass right over objects smaller than 250 feet across and are reflected back only from very big obstacles, such as large ships or undersea mounts. (As anyone who's been anywhere near a rock concert knows, the other thing that affects how far a sound travels is its loudness. On this point, whales can outdo rock musicians and even jet aircraft. A blue whale is the loudest creature on earth, able to produce a pulse of 188 decibels.)

High-frequency sounds, on the other hand, with wavelengths of one-hundredth of an inch (0.02 cm) or less, can be deflected from their path by the smallest obstruction. Because these short waves are unlikely to get very far without hitting something, they are of limited use for communication but excellent for sonar.

The sonar system of some cetaceans is remarkably sophisticated. Some species can flatten or heighten their sound beams to help them focus on a target, and some can even send out two different frequencies in two different directions at the same time. Typically, an Odontocete such as a dolphin sends out bursts of clicks at regular intervals to monitor its surroundings, altering the frequency up or down as needed to build up a picture of what is around it. If something interesting appears on its sonar, the dolphin can shift to a steady stream of ultra-high-frequency sounds to provide high-resolution detail.

By listening to the returning echoes, an Odontocete can tell how far away something is, how big it is, its texture, whether it is moving, and other details. Using ultrasound alone, a blindfolded dolphin in captivity can distinguish among a metal square, a wooden square, and a plastic square of identical sizes placed 100 feet (30 m) away. It can detect wires finer than 0.015 inches (0.038 cm) in diameter and tell one ball from another so similar in size that experimenters have to measure them to see the difference. With this fabulous sense, a toothed whale will easily know which species of fish are ahead, even in total darkness.

The audible notes whales use to communicate with one another are no less interesting than their sonar sounds. Many whales can be recognized as individuals from the particular noises they make, perhaps the best known being the "singing" humpbacks. These remarkable animals create the longest and most complex calls known in the animal kingdom, combining chirps, whistles, rumbles, and other sounds into sequences to form "songs" that may last from six minutes to half an hour. Humpbacks often sing over periods of many hours, warbling a series of songs separated by brief pauses.

Each population of humpbacks develops songs with characteristic patterns, different from those of other populations. Their songs evolve a little from year to year, but all the whales living in one area incorporate the changes to maintain a consistent local dialect.

Humpbacks sing mainly in the breeding season, and it is usually solitary males who sing. This suggests that their songs are serenades, meaning "I'm here, strong and healthy, ready to mate"; but the complexity of the performances hint that there's more to them than that.

Studies of the sounds made by orcas show the subtlety and variety of whale language. Orcas use discrete calls – distinct sounds separated into characteristic types that can be heard as much as 5 miles (8 km) away – to maintain contact with each other and keep the groups together. When hunting, they call in irregular bursts with long pauses in between. When traveling in large numbers, orcas call more often – 50 times or more per minute. Small groups traveling in tight formation may be completely silent, however.

Like humpbacks, each population of orcas has its own repertoire of discrete calls. Different pods have different sounds, recognizable even to human ears. Pods of resident orcas in the Pacific northwest use between 7 and 17 calls each, while pods of transients have smaller vocabularies of between 4 and 7 discrete calls, each distinctly different from those of residents.

Orcas make noises of quite another sort when playing or socializing. Unlike the clear notes of discrete calls, the sounds of playful orcas are random, variable, boisterous, and noisy. It's like the difference between a group of neighborhood dogs barking in their backyards, and the same group whining, yelping, yipping, howling, and growling when taken out to play together in the park.

What is a language? How does human language differ from, say, bird song or the dance patterns that bees use to communicate? There's much debate over the answers, but on any criteria the sounds that whales make to one another are not simply repetitive, instinctive, or rigid. Scientists can tell what relationship one whale has with another by analyzing their vocalizations. Intriguingly, an orca placed in captivity with another caught an ocean away will learn to use the dialect of its new companion. As with so many other mysteries surrounding whales, we must wait for more research to enlighten us on this subject.

While the ocean environment directed the evolution of hearing as the cetaceans' most important sense, it also molded the bodies of whales, adapting them to survival under water. Their streamlined shapes and smooth skins are designed, like the hulls of ships, to reduce drag. For such big creatures, their skins are relatively thin: the epidermis and dermis together are no thicker than 2.5 inches (6.3 cm) in even the largest whales. They don't need protecting against wind, rain, thorns, dust, and other wear and tear, and are very sensitive to touch.

Anyone who has got close enough to a cetacean to pat it or stroke it knows the feel of that firm, rubbery, smooth-as-glass skin – a bit like the inflated inner tube of a bicycle tire. Whales and dolphins in captivity appear to enjoy being petted, and in the wild they often rub against one another, especially during courtship. On the east coast of Vancouver Island is a shallow bay where orcas regularly come to rub themselves against a pebbly beach; no one knows why. The skins of whales lack hair and the glands that produce sweat and oil in other mammals – they normally have no need of them. If stranded and exposed to air, whales quickly dry out and get sunburned, having no protection against such unfamiliar threats.

Beneath the skin is a layer of fat or blubber, ranging in thickness from an inch (2.5 cm) or so in tropical porpoises to more than a foot (0.3 m) in species that live in cold water. As warm-blooded mammals, whales generate heat from inside and have a high metabolism, like a furnace set on high. Their blubber insulates them, slowing the escape of body heat into the surrounding water. A bowhead whale's 20 tons (18 t) of blubber keep it warm even in near-freezing Arctic waters, where it lives year-round.

Blubber has other functions, too. It is a reservoir of stored food, supplying energy for prolonged activity or during periods of fasting. Blubber also affects the density of the whale's body, giving it buoyancy and so reducing the energy needed to swim near the surface.

The skeleton of a whale, similarly, is designed for life in water. It is generally much lighter than the skeleton of a similar-sized land animal would be, and forms no more than 17 percent of the body weight of even the largest whales. Its function is not so much to support weight as to provide an anchor for the muscles.

Whale bone consists of a thin shell of compact outer material covering a spongy inner structure. The large spaces within the bone are filled with a fatty marrow, which makes up as much as a third of the total oil yielded by a whale's body. Their spongy, fatty structure gives whale bones a low density, and they are able to float on water.

The biggest share of a whale's body goes to muscle, which makes up about 40 percent of the total mass. Powerful enough to propel the leviathan through the seas, the tightly packed muscle fibers are nearly as strong as steel. A whale can be suspended out of water by its tail flukes without their breaking. The greatest bulk of muscle is, in fact, along the tail and lower back, which provide the thrust for movement.

Unlike fish, which have vertical tail fins that they wave from side to side, whales move by stroking their horizontal flukes up and down. They have supple backbones and flexible tails, belying their rigid-looking, torpedo-like body shape. Pushing with their flukes against the water, whales develop tremendous force from their muscles – enough, for example, to propel a 5-ton (4.5-t) orca more than 20 feet (6 m) into the air. In water, orcas have been clocked at speeds of more than 20 knots (23 nautical miles or 36.8 km per hour) when chasing prey. Even large baleen whales are able to get up speeds of 20 knots for short periods. Studies on dolphins show that they increase their swimming speed by vibrating their skins, reducing the drag set up by turbulence.

A whale's flippers are not used for propulsion, but for steering and balance. They are smooth and rounded, like paddles. Inside each flipper are bones arranged much as they are in your hand, with four or five fingers – more evidence of the whales' origin on land. The dorsal fin does not have bones in it, and not all whales have dorsal fins. One of the most impressive is the nearly 6-foot

(1.8-m)-long dorsal fin of a bull orca, which may function as a symbol of status, like the antlers of an elk or the tail of a peacock.

There's another very practical use that fins may have. It has to do with heat control. While its high metabolism and insulating blubber are very good at keeping a whale warm, there is a down side: the whale is like someone permanently wearing a heavy overcoat. What to do when it gets *too* warm – after a long chase, say? The whale can't shed its blubber, and it can't sweat as we do, or pant like a dog. What it does is shunt warm blood into its fins. Thin and lacking blubber, but with plenty of blood vessels, the fins act like radiators, quickly getting rid of excess body heat into the surrounding air or water.

Finding food under water, but still dependent on air, cetaceans have developed special adaptations for diving. One we have already seen is the blowhole. A single slit in toothed whales and a pair of holes in baleen whales, the blowhole is opened only for breathing. Muscular elastic lips keep it tightly closed whenever the whale submerges. The position of the blowhole on top of the whale allows the animal to breathe while most of its body remains below the surface.

The blowhole is connected directly to the lungs, bypassing the whale's mouth. This separation of air and food passages allows the whale to feed at depth without the risk of having water forced into its lungs. There is no system of nasal passages (except for Odontocetes, which have a very complex system), as in land mammals, to filter dust and to warm and moisten the air, because sea air is already clean and moist.

Surprisingly, perhaps, whales do not have particularly large lungs. At most, they are less than 3 percent of a whale's body weight; a human's lungs are more than twice that. The difference is that whales use their lungs very efficiently. We take in only a small fraction of our lungs' capacity when we inhale, but a whale completely fills its lungs and changes up to 90 percent of its air supply with each breath. Whales expel used air with gusto, shooting it from their blowholes at speeds of between 100 and 300 miles (160 and 480 km) per hour in powerful bursts lasting little more than half a second each. They draw in fresh air with equal vigor, inhaling up to 3,000 times the volume of air we do in about 1 second.

To prepare for diving, a whale takes several deep breaths, building up the supply of oxygen in its body. As well as storing dissolved oxygen in its blood, as we do, a whale also carries a huge reserve of this vital gas in its muscles.

Whales dive mainly to find food. Baleen whales, whose food drifts near the surface, rarely dive deeply or for very long. They can go for a 5- or 10-minute dive after taking only 3 or 4 breaths. Sperm whales, however, frequently descend for 30 minutes to an hour at a time in pursuit of squid. They spend longer periods breathing at the surface before a dive, taking about one breath for each minute they will spend under water.

Deep divers face the problems of pressure. For human divers, the biggest threats are compression at great depth and, when they ascend, the "bends" – excruciating pain caused when dissolved nitrogen in their blood vessels turns back into bubbles of gas as pressure is reduced. Whales avoid these problems simply because their lungs collapse under high pressure. This forces the air from their lungs into their windpipes and nasal passages, and there it cannot be absorbed into the body. They continue to survive on the large amounts of oxygen already stored in their blood and muscles.

Understanding how animals can be so different from one another and yet so similar is one of the sublime revelations in the concept of evolution. The basic body structures of a whale and a human are, to a zoologist, not so very unlike. Both have similar patterns of bones, muscles, organs, and blood. Both have eyes and ears, brains and hearts. Whales and people resemble each other much more closely than either resembles, say, a snail. Yet this common body structure is adapted in the whale for a life under water, while in us it has evolved to suit a very different environment.

RIGHT: SOLITARY MALE HUMPBACKS ARE CHAMPION "SINGERS," PRODUCING LONG AND COMPLEX SERIES OF SOUNDS OVER MANY HOURS. THE FUNCTION, IF ANY, OF THESE "SONGS" ISN'T KNOWN, ALTHOUGH THEY MAY HELP A WHALE ATTRACT A MATE.

OPPOSITE: A WHALE'S SENSE OF VISION IS LIMITED BY THE MURKINESS OF THE OCEAN. SOUND IS GENERALLY MUCH MORE IMPORTANT TO WHALES THAN SIGHT.

🐋

RIGHT: WHALES OFTEN STAND WITH THEIR HEADS LIFTED CLEAR OF THE WATER TO GET A BETTER LOOK WHEN A BOAT APPROACHES THEM. THEY CAN MAINTAIN THIS POSITION FOR AS LONG AS 30 SECONDS, OFTEN TURNING IN A FULL CIRCLE TO SCAN THEIR SURROUNDINGS.

LEFT: A DIVER INVESTIGATES THE HUGE VERTEBRAE THAT MAKE UP A WHALE'S BACKBONE. POWERFUL TAIL MUSCLES ATTACHED TO THE VERTEBRAE OF THE LOWER BACK PROVIDE THE THRUST THAT PROPELS A WHALE THROUGH THE WATER.

OPPOSITE: AN UPSIDE-DOWN HUMPBACK WAVES ITS LONG FLIPPERS ABOVE THE SEA SURFACE. INSIDE THE WHALE'S FLIPPERS ARE THE SAME BASIC SET OF ARM, WRIST, AND FINGER BONES FOUND IN MOST MAMMALS.

LEFT: SOME WHALES CAN SUBMERGE FOR MORE THAN AN HOUR AT A

TIME, SURVIVING ON A SINGLE LUNGFUL OF AIR. DESPITE THIS FACT,

THEIR LUNGS ARE NOT PARTICULARLY LARGE. THE SECRET LIES IN THE

ABILITY OF THEIR MUSCLES TO HOLD DISSOLVED OXYGEN.

ABOVE: WHALES ARE PROPELLED COMPLETELY BY THEIR TAILS. A

WHALE SWIMMING UNDERWATER CAN SOMETIMES BE TRACKED ON A

CALM SEA BY THE SURGES OF WATER THAT SPILL UP TO THE SURFACE

AS IT STROKES ITS BROAD TAIL FLUKES UP AND DOWN.

75

THE BLOWHOLE OF A WHALE IS SURROUNDED BY THICK, MUSCULAR LIPS THAT CLOSE TIGHTLY WHEN THE WHALE DIVES. A RAISED

RIDGE AROUND THE BLOWHOLE PREVENTS ACCIDENTAL FLOODING WHILE THE WHALE IS BREATHING ON THE SURFACE.

RIGHT: THE TIME THAT A WHALE SPENDS ON THE SURFACE TO BREATHE DEPENDS PARTLY ON THE DURATION OF ITS DIVES. MOST BALEEN WHALES DO NOT DIVE VERY DEEP OR FOR VERY LONG, AND TWO OR THREE BREATHS ARE ENOUGH TO REPLENISH THEIR OXYGEN.

🐋

BELOW: A FIN WHALE BREAKS THE SURFACE TO BREATHE. FIN WHALES ARE FOUND IN ALL OCEANS AND SOMETIMES CONGREGATE IN GROUPS OF 100 OR MORE IN THEIR FAVORITE FEEDING GROUNDS.

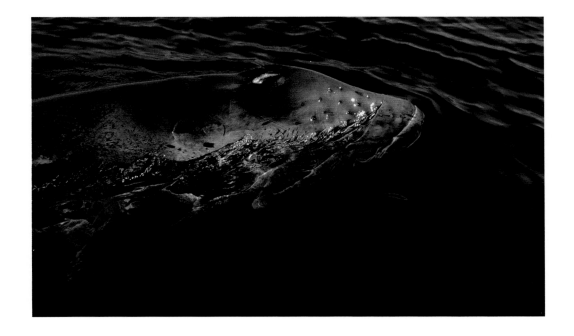

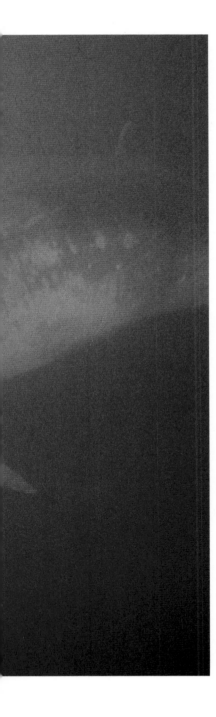

SECOND ONLY TO BLUE WHALES IN LENGTH AND WEIGHT, FIN WHALES ARE THE FASTEST OF THE GREAT

WHALES, SWIMMING AT SPEEDS OF MORE THAN 20 KNOTS (UP TO 40 KM PER HOUR).

LOOKING LIKE AN AIRSHIP SOARING THROUGH A STARRY SKY, A STREAMLINED BLUE WHALE

CRUISES ON THE SURFACE OF A SPARKLING OCEAN. ITS LONG, TORPEDO-SHAPED BODY

HELPS IT MOVE UNDERWATER, AND A THICK LAYER OF BLUBBER BENEATH THE SKIN KEEPS

IT WARM IN THE FRIGID OCEANS WHERE IT FEEDS.

PUSHING WITH ITS TAIL FLUKES AGAINST THE WATER, A FULL-GROWN ORCA CAN

LAUNCH ITSELF MORE THAN 20 FEET (6 M) INTO THE AIR.

SCIENTISTS MONITOR WHALE SOUNDS USING UNDERWATER MICROPHONES,

WHILE A CURIOUS WHALE BREAKS THE SURFACE NEARBY.

SEA LIONS, SEALS, AND WALRUS ARE OTHER MAMMALS
ADAPTED TO LIVE IN THE SEA. UNLIKE WHALES, SEA
LIONS PROPEL THEMSELVES WITH THEIR FRONT FLIPPERS,
USING THEIR WEBBED REAR FEET AS RUDDERS.

AFTER 12 MONTHS OF GESTATION, A HUMPBACK WHALE PRODUCES

A 15-FOOT (4.5-M)-LONG CALF WEIGHING ABOUT 1 1/2 TONS (1.5 T).

SHE MAY MATE AGAIN SOON AFTER GIVING BIRTH.

RIGHT: A MOTHER HUMPBACK IS VERY PROTECTIVE OF

HER CALF. ONE MOTHER WAS SEEN TAKING HER YOUNG CALF

UNDER A FLIPPER WHEN THEY WERE THREATENED.

ABOVE: A PAIR OF SPOTTED DOLPHINS FROLIC NEAR THE

BAHAMAS. CALVES ARE BORN WITHOUT SPOTS AND

SLOWLY DEVELOP THEM ALONG THEIR BODIES BETWEEN

ONE AND TWO YEARS OF AGE.

ABOVE: NARWHALS MIGRATE ALONG THE ARCTIC COASTLINES, FOLLOWING THE SEASONAL MOVEMENTS OF THE ICEPACK. DURING THE MATING SEASON IN EARLY SPRING, ADULT MALES WILL COMPETE TO MATE WITH FEMALES.

❧

OPPOSITE: A NARWHAL DISPLAYS HIS SPLENDID TUSK, A SPIRAL TOOTH THAT GROWS OUT THROUGH A HOLE IN HIS UPPER LIP. FEMALE NARWHALS DO NOT HAVE TUSKS, WHICH PROBABLY SERVE AS SYMBOLS OF MASCULINITY DURING COURTSHIP AND AGGRESSIVE DISPLAYS.

BOTH MALE AND FEMALE ORCAS
LIVE IN A SOCIAL GROUP WITH
THEIR MOTHERS THROUGHOUT
THEIR LIVES.

SAVING THE WHALES

THE ROLL CALL IS MOURNFUL. BLUE WHALE: more than 200,000 in 1900, fewer than 12,000 today. Bowhead whale: once abundant, now in scattered populations totaling fewer than 6,000. Humpback whale: once in the hundreds of thousands, fewer than 8,000 today. Narwhal: fewer than 20,000 and declining. Right whale: once abundant, now numbering under 2,000.

Rare. Endangered. Declining.

Since the heyday of whaling ships in the 1800s, and continuing still in the present, the world has witnessed our shameful overexploitation of whales and the sad decline of one species after another.

It's ironic that most of our knowledge about cetaceans before the last 30 years came from whalers. It was part of their trade to know the numbers, sizes, and distribution of different species. They knew for how long a particular whale might disappear on a dive, and where it might resurface. They could identify whales from their blowspouts and knew how fast they could swim – faster when being

LEFT: TANGLED IN AN ABANDONED FISHING NET, A WHALE EXPERIENCES ONE OF THE MANY THREATS TO ITS LIFE CAUSED BY HUMANS. OTHERS INCLUDE OIL SPILLS, FLOATING JUNK, POLLUTION, AND OVERFISHING.

pursued. They took grisly advantage of the fact that whales often approach to help a member of their herd in distress.

Throughout the 1700s and 1800s, whale meat, oil, and baleen were prized materials, used in hundreds of products, and whalers from many nations took to the seas in search of their valuable quarry. Their tools were sailing ships, rowboats, harpoons, skill, experience, and courage. The whalers thrived, and by 1850 the U.S. whaling industry alone employed more than 700 vessels for the purpose of killing sperm whales.

Around the start of this century, new technologies began to appear. They provided materials and products that could replace many of those previously supplied only by whales. But they also brought changes that would have more terrible impacts on whales than ever before.

According to one report, modern whalers killed more whales during the 50 years from 1920 to 1970 than in the entire bloody history of whaling in the preceding four centuries. Thirty thousand blue whales were killed in the Antarctic in a single season (1930–31), and another 63,000 whales were killed in 1964 alone. High-speed diesel engines, sonar, and explosives made the slaughter possible. Human greed and indifference allowed it to happen.

By the 1930s, it was obvious that the uncontrolled taking of whales could not continue indefinitely. Studies were initiated to collect information about the whale species that were under the most pressure. How many were left? What were their age and sex ratios? How quickly did they reproduce? Were their remaining populations viable?

Answers to these questions are not always clear even today. Early population projections were based as much on mathematical models as on actual field data.

And some of the models themselves were influenced by data from fisheries, ignoring the fact that fish and cetaceans are very different creatures.

The survival of whale populations is not a question of numbers alone. The capture of individuals leaves remaining members of a herd having to restructure their social groups. The death of a key animal – such as a mature mother or a breeding bull – may affect the success of its relatives. Research shows that whales, like some other social mammals, can respond to hunting pressure by growing faster and maturing and breeding at younger ages, but such changes may also take their toll.

In the 1940s, the International Whaling Commission (IWC) was established to encourage research and to try to regulate the whaling business. The IWC sets whaling seasons, defines areas where ships may hunt, authorizes the minimum size of animals that may be caught, and limits the total numbers caught. It also declares some species totally protected, but its guidelines are not always followed. Into the 1990s, Japan, Iceland, and Norway are keeping up pressure to continue their killing of whales.

With the 1970s came a sea change in popular attitudes toward whales. Better undersea films showed these gentle and playful creatures to the public in their natural state, rather than at the wrong end of a harpoon. More and more people saw some of the smaller whales for themselves, as captive dolphins went through their tricks at newly opened seaquariums. There were TV programs featuring heroic dolphins, and the songs of humpback whales were recorded and issued for sale on records.

All these things revealed the beauty and intelligence of whales, creating interest in them and raising concerns for their survival in the wild. Support for more research grew, and scientists developed techniques for studying cetaceans at sea. Using photographs, sound recordings, and radio transmitters, they began identifying individual animals and tracking them over long periods of time. Their findings were a big step for humankind in our knowledge of whales. We were able, at last, to learn something of the nature of whales without killing or molesting them.

While some researchers were following cetaceans in boats, others were probing the capabilities of whales and dolphins in captivity. One researcher during the 1960s, Dr. John Lilly, carried attempts at interspecies communication the furthest. He even conducted an experiment in which a woman and a dolphin lived together constantly for several months. After 10 years of research, however, Lilly closed his lab, feeling he could no longer keep such complex and social animals in captivity.

The view of whales as self-conscious creatures like ourselves became widespread. Captive dolphins and orcas had been effective ambassadors for their kind, but now some people have begun to question the ethics of capturing and keeping these animals for any purpose.

Perhaps more than any other species, orcas turned public thinking around. The name and reputation of the "killer whale" suggests an animal of tigerlike ferocity. Imagine people's puzzlement, then, when captured orcas turned out to be as docile and lovable as lambs. These 6-ton (5.4-t) monsters, their mouths studded with large, pointed teeth, quickly learned to rise from the water in their pools and kiss their keepers' offered cheeks with the utmost gentleness.

The restraint these powerful animals show toward humans is one of their most puzzling characteristics. Wild orcas are indeed formidable predators that hunt and kill any warm-blooded mammal in their path. Yet there has never been an authentic report of an orca killing, or even harming, a human except under provocation or by accident. Trainers in marine shows once commonly rode the backs of captive orcas and put their heads inside those massive jaws. Filmmakers producing a wildlife documentary have even swum unharmed among wild orcas that were hunting seals. Why orcas exclude humans from their menu is a mystery, and it is regrettable that we do not return the favor. Until very recently, and perhaps on occasion still today, orcas were commonly shot or dynamited by fishermen as vermin.

The debate over captive whales and dolphins continues. There is money to be made from them, and there are arguments, too, that these animals further the causes of education, research, and conservation. Captive whales and dolphins have been bred in captivity. Breeding adults often suffer from lack of experience in raising young, and do not have the social support and stimulation they would get in the wild. Confinement may also increase the risk of poor health and infection. It is almost impossible to confine to a pool a very intelligent and social animal weighing 4 tons (3.6 t) and used to swimming 50 miles (80 km) each day, and prevent it from experiencing problems of boredom and stress.

As much of a threat as whaling, the effects of habitat degradation are appearing today in oceans around the world. Oil spills, air and water pollution, and overfishing are only the most obvious problems. Whales are directly affected by being tangled in abandoned drift nets, or eating floating junk. They are indirectly affected by poisons that wash from the land, down rivers, and into the sea – poisons that enter the bodies of fish eaten by whales, accumulate in the whales' fatty tissues, and are passed to the newborns of the next generation in their mothers' milk.

The links connecting the fates of people and whales can be even more subtle. For example, logging in the steep valleys of the Pacific northwest disrupts watersheds, sending eroded mud and gravel down denuded slopes and into the river systems that are the spawning grounds of Pacific salmon. The silt in the water smothers fish eggs and fry, and the loss of overhanging forest shade allows the rivers to grow warmer, putting stress on all manner of river life. Salmon – the food of orcas – decline in numbers as a result. Thus, logging adversely affects whales.

Perhaps the biggest tragedy of all is that we still understand so little about most whale species. Even the lists of information about such basic data as growth rates, longevity, distribution, and population size are filled with the melancholy admission: "unknown." And details of courtship, hunting, and daily routines have never been observed or described for some species. What *is* known, however, is that whales of most species today are drastically rarer than they were earlier in this century, in some cases having lost as much as 90 percent of their former numbers.

The opportunities for whale watchers in the 1990s are a shadow of what was available to our great-grandparents. The irony is that more people now have the wealth and leisure to travel than in the past, but there is less splendor in the natural world for people to see. We can still, however, go out on ships today and see whales as they have lived in the oceans for millions of years. Whether future generations will have that chance is in our hands alone: there can be no excuses.

ABOVE: ABOUT HALF THE WORLD'S CETACEANS ARE VARIOUS SPECIES OF DOLPHINS OR PORPOISES. MOST LIVE IN WARMER OCEANS, AND A FEW SPECIES ARE FOUND IN LARGE RIVERS.

INSET: PERFORMING DOLPHINS IN AQUARIUMS AND MOVIES FIRST SHOWED THE PUBLIC AT LARGE THE INTELLIGENCE AND GRACE SHARED BY OTHER CETACEANS.

OPPOSITE: A DEAD HUMPBACK IS

TOWED AWAY FROM A BEACH FOR

BURIAL AT SEA.

❧

RIGHT: A FISHERY OFFICER TAKES

TISSUE SAMPLES FROM A STRANDED

GRAY WHALE TO DISCOVER THE

CAUSE OF ITS DEATH.

ABOVE: INUIT HUNTERS TRADITIONALLY FOUND BELUGAS BY WAITING FOR THEM BESIDE

ISOLATED HOLES IN THE ICE WHERE THE WHALES WERE FORCED TO BREATHE.

❧

OPPOSITE: THE NAME OF THE PILOT WHALE MAY COME FROM THEIR HABIT OF SWIM-

MING IN LINE, FOLLOWING ONE IN THE LEAD. GROUPS ARE SO CLOSELY BONDED THAT

IF ONE WHALE IS STRANDED, THE WHOLE GROUP WILL FOLLOW IT ONTO THE BEACH.

AS MANY AS SEVERAL HUNDRED HAVE BEEN FOUND STRANDED TOGETHER.

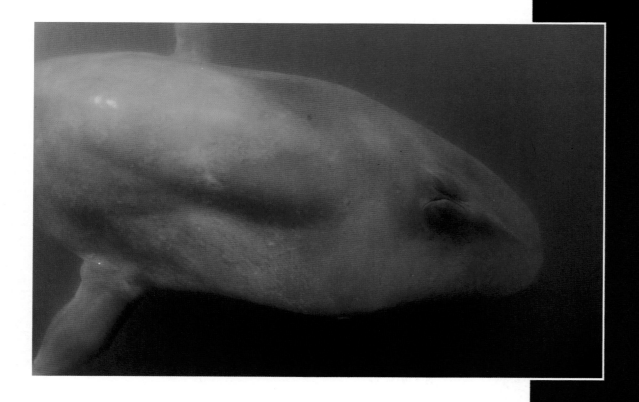

ABOVE: LIKE MOST OF THE WORLD'S CETACEANS, BLUE

WHALES STILL HOLD MANY SECRETS FROM HUMAN

INVESTIGATORS. THE DIFFICULTY OF OBSERVING EVEN

SUCH LARGE ANIMALS IN THE VAST EXPANSE OF THE

OCEANS MEANS THAT WE STILL KNOW VERY LITTLE

ABOUT THEM.

❧

RIGHT: THE LARGEST ANIMALS EVER TO HAVE LIVED ON

EARTH, BLUE WHALES ARE IN DANGER OF EXTINCTION

AS A RESULT OF HUMAN GREED AND INDIFFERENCE.

116

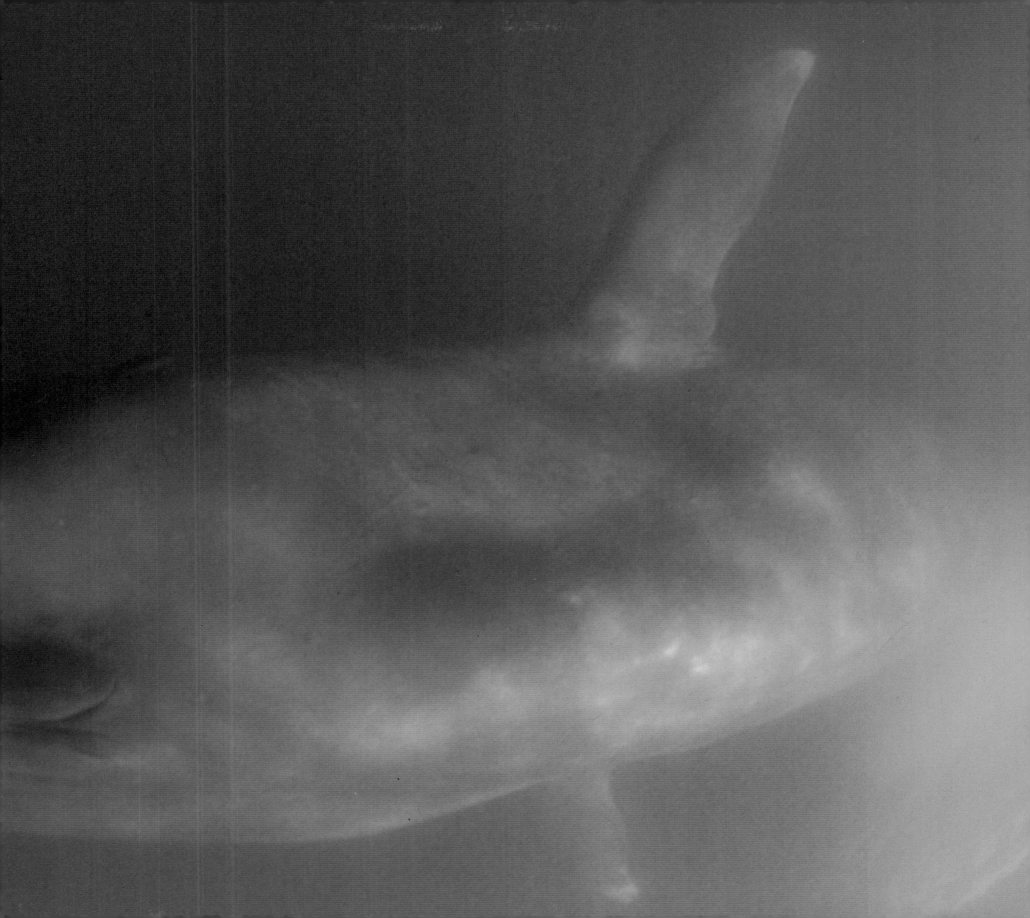

RIGHT: THE LAST VIEW OF A WHALE.

🐋

OPPOSITE: A BOWHEAD WHALE SHOWS

THE CHARACTERISTIC WHITE "BIB" ON

ITS CHIN. BOWHEADS ARE THE ONLY

LARGE WHALES LIVING YEAR-ROUND

IN THE ARCTIC. ONCE EXTREMELY

COMMON, BOWHEADS NOW NUMBER

PROBABLY FEWER THAN 3,000

THROUGHOUT THE WORLD.

FAMILIES OF WHALES

BALEEN WHALES (MYSTICETI)

Right whales (Balaenidae)
  Right
  Bowhead
  Pygmy right

Rorquals (Balaenopteridae)
  Blue
  Fin
  Sei
  Bryde's
  Piked (Minke)
  Humpback

Gray whale (Eschrichtiidae)
  Gray

TOOTHED WHALES (ODONTOCETI)

Beaked whales (Ziphiidae)
  18 species of beaked and
  bottlenose whales

River dolphins (Platanistidae)
  Ganges River
  Indus River
  Yangtse River
  Amazon River
  La Plata River

Narwhal and Beluga (Monodontidae)
  Narwhal (Unicorn whale)
  Beluga (White whale)

Sperm whales (Physeteridae)
  Sperm
  Pygmy sperm
  Dwarf sperm

Porpoises (Phocoenidae)
  Common
  Black
  Spectacled
  Gulf
  Finless
  Spray (Dall's)

Dolphins (Delphinidae)
  26 species of dolphins

Pilot whales and killer whales
(Globicephalidae)
  Longfin pilot
  Shortfin pilot
  Killer
  False killer
  Pygmy killer
  Melonhead

CONSERVATION GROUPS

Porpoise Rescue Foundation
2040 Harbour Drive, Ste. 101
San Diego, CA 92101
(619) 574-1573

Pacific Whale Foundation
Kealia Beach Plaza, Ste. 25
101 N. Kihei Road
Kealia, HI 96753
(808) 879-8811

Whale Adoption Project
70 East Falmouth Highway
East Falmouth, MA 02536
(508) 548-8328

Sea Shepherd Conservation Society
3107A Washington Boulevard
Marina del Rey, CA 90292
(310) 301-7325

Cetacean Society International
P.O. Box 343
Plainville, CT 06062-8400
(203) 793-8400

Wildlife Preservation Trust International
3400 West Girard Avenue
Philadelphia, PA 19104
(215) 222-3636

Endangered Species Coalition
666 Pennsylvania Avenue S.E.
Washington, DC 20003
(202) 547-9009

Defenders of Wildlife
1244 19th Street N.W.
Washington, DC 20036
(202) 659-9510

SELECTED BIBLIOGRAPHY

Bulloch, David K. *The Whale Watcher's Handbook*. New York: Lyons and Burford, 1993.

Connor, Richard C. and Peterson, Dawn. *The Lives of Whales and Dolphins*. New York: Henry Holt and Co., 1994.

Ellis, Richard. *The Book of Whales*. New York: Alfred A. Knopf, 1980.

Ellis, Richard. *Men and Whales*. New York: Alfred A. Knopf, 1991.

Gaskin, D. E. *The Ecology of Whales and Dolphins*. London: Heinemann, 1982.

Gatenby, Greg, ed. *Whales: A Celebration*. Toronto: Little, Brown and Co., 1983.

Golden, Frederic. "Whither the Whales." *Oceanus* 32, no. 1 (Spring 1989).

Heimlich-Boran, Sara and James. *Killer Whales*. Stillwater, MN: Voyageur Press, 1994.

Heintzelman, Donald S. *A World Guide to Whales, Dolphins and Porpoises*. Tulsa: Winchester Press, 1981.

Leatherwood, Stephen and Reeves, Randall R. *The Sierra Club Handbook of Whales and Dolphins*. San Francisco, Sierra Club Books, 1983.

Lilly, John C. *Lilly on Dolphins*. Garden City: Anchor Books, 1975.

Norris, Kenneth S. *Dolphin Days*. New York: W. W. Norton and Co., 1991.

Payne, Roger, ed. *Communication and Behavior of Whales*. Boulder: Westview Press Inc., 1983.

Pryor, Karen and Norris, Kenneth S. *Dolphin Societies: Discoveries and Puzzles*. Berkeley: University of California Press, 1991.

Robson, Frank D. *Strandings: Ways to Save Whales*. Johannesburg: The Science Press, 1984.

Tillman, M. F. and Donovan, G. P., eds. *Special Issue on Historical Whaling Records*. Cambridge: International Whaling Commission, 1983.

Watson, Lyall. *Sea Guide to Whales of the World*. New York: E. P. Dutton, 1981.

Winn, Lois King and Winn, Howard E. *Wings in the Sea: The Humpback Whale*. Hanover: University Press of New England, 1985.

PHOTOGRAPHY CREDITS

INDEX

Note: Page numbers in italics indicate photographs.

Anatomy, 14-15, 59-60, 63-65
    of sperm whale, 38
Antarctic, 39-40, 86, 106
Arctic, *23*, 39, 64, 86, *98*, *118*

Bahamas, *96*
Baleen, about, 35
Baleen whale, 34, 39-41, 67
Beaked whale, 15, 38
Behaviour patterns, orca, 37
Beluga whale, *23*, *56-57*
Biological productivity of oceans, 39-40
Birth, 85-87
Blowhole, 66-67, *76*
Blowspout, 13-15
Blubber, 64
Blue whale, 16, 34, 40, *55*, 60, *80*, *84-85*, 86, 88
    feeding, *48*
    population decline, 105-106, *116-117*
Bone, whale, 64-65
Bowhead whale, 34, 64, 105, *118*
Breaching, 16-17, *20-21*, *55*
Breathing, *75*, *76*, *77*
Breeding, 88, 89
Breeding season, 88
    and songs, 62
British Columbia, 36

Calves, 39, 86-90, *92-93*, *94-95*, *96-97*

Captive whales, 108-109
Cetacean order, 15, 61, 107
Communication, 18, 60-63
    interspecies, 108
Courtship, 64, 88
Croaker fish, 57

Diving:
    adaptation for, 66-68
    and sperm whale, 38
Dolphin family, *30*
Dolphin, 15-16, *96*, 107, *111*
Dorsal fin, *28*, *31*, *52*, 65-66, *101*

Ear opening, 59
Echolocation, 59, 60
Evolution of whales, 14
Extinction, danger of, *116-117*

False killer whale, *31*
Families of whales, 122
Family life, 88-92
Feeding, of calves, 87
Feeding habits, 35, 39-41
    Odontocetes, 35
    orca, 36-37
    sexual differences, 39
Fin whale, 34, 77, *78-79*
Flippers, 23-24, 65, *73*
Food, 15, 33
    animal protein in Antarctic waters, 40
    See also Krill; Plankton
Food gathering techniques, 34-36

Food-finding, and sound frequency, 60

Gestation, 85, 88, 91
Gray whale, 15, 17, 18, *24*, *42*, *44*, *49*, *113*
    feeding habits, 35

Habitat degradation, 109
Hawaii, 13
Hearing, sense of, 58
Human threat to, 104-106, 110
Humpback whale, 15-16, *20-21*, 23-24, 29, *50-51*, *94-95*, *96-97*, 105, *112*
    feeding, 34-35, *46-47*, *54-55*
    songs of, 62, *69*, 107
Hunters:
    sense of sound for seeing, 58-59
    species of, 35-39
Hunting grounds, 36

Iceland, 107
Intelligence, 17, *111*
International Whaling Commission (IWC), 107
Inuit hunters, *114*

Japan, 107

Killer whale. *See* Orca
Krill, 40, *47*

Language, of whales, 62-63
Lifespan, 17, 88, 90
Lilly, John, 108

Long-beaked dolphin, 36
Lungs, 66-68, *75*

Mammals, 13-15, 64
Mating, 84-86, 89-91, *100*
Maui, 15
Melon, 59
Melonhead whale, *31*
Migration, 15, 39, 86, *98*
Minke whale, *52*
Mouth, 33-34
Mustache, whales with a, 34
Mysticetes, 34

Narwhal, 91, *99*, 105
Navigation, and sound frequency, 60
Noise, underwater, 57
Norway, 36, 107

Odontocetes, 35, 36, 58-59, 61
Orca, *12-13*, *32-33*, *42-43*, *81*, 108-109
    family life, 88-90, *101-102*
        feeding habits, 35-37
        language of, 62-63
Ovulation, 88

Pacific coast, 36
Pacific northwest, 36-37
Pilot whale, 15, *28*, *30*, *115*
Plankton, 33, 39-41
Play, 17, 18, 63, 87-88, 91
Pods, 89, *101*
    language of, 62-63

Polar regions, 39
Pollution, 109-110
Population decline, 105, 110
Porpoise, 15-16, *111*
Predators, 33
Pygmy killer whale, *50-51*, 53

Resident orca, 37, 62, 89
Right whale, 16, 34, 105
Rorqual whale, 34, *45*
    See also Baleen whale; Blue whale

Sea canaries, 57
Sea lion, *26-27*, *32-33*, *83*
Seals, *26*
Seaquariums, 107
Sei whale, 34
Sensory system, 58
Sexual behaviour, 91-92
Sexual maturity, 89-90, 91
Sight, sense of, 58, *71*
Size, 16, 91
    of calves, 87, *94-95*
Skeleton, 64
Skin, of the whale, 64
Smell, sense of, 58
Social behaviour, orca, 37, 63
Social organization, 17, 88-92, *103*, 107
Sonar system, 59, 61
Songs, of whales, 62, *69*
Sound:
    frequency, 60-61
    use of for seeing, 57-63, *71*, *82*

Sound waves, 59
Speed, 38
Swimming, 65
Sperm whale, 16, 35, 59, 106
    as divers, 38, 67
    family life, 90-92
Squid, as food, 37-38

Taste, sense of, 58
Technology, and whale-killing, 106
Teeth:
    of hunters, 35-36
    of orca, *42-43*
Throat, of rorqual, *45*
Transient orca, 37, 63
Tropical waters, 86

Ultrasound, 61

Vancouver (City), *44*
Vancouver Island, *12-13*
Vertebrae, of whale's backbone, 72
Vision. *See* Sight
Vocal communication, 18

Walrus, *26*
Washington (State), 36
Whale watchers, *19*, *25*
Whalers, 105-106
Whaling industry, 106
White whale, *56-57*